C000185078

the little book of
WELLNESS

vicki vrint

summersdale

THE LITTLE BOOK OF WELLNESS

An Hachette UK Company
www.hachette.co.uk

Summersdale Publishers Ltd
Part of Octopus Publishing Group Limited
Carmelite House
50 Victoria Embankment
LONDON
EC4Y 0DZ
UK

www.summersdale.com

Printed and bound in the Czech Republic

ISBN: 978-1-78783-236-7

Substantial discounts on bulk quantities of Summersdale books are available to corporations, professional associations and other organizations. For details contact general enquiries: telephone: +44 (0) 1243 771107 or email: enquiries@summersdale.com.

INTRODUCTION

You might be wondering what exactly we mean when we speak of "wellness". It's definitely a term that's growing in popularity these days, but it helps to be clear about the concept: it doesn't just refer to an absence of bodily pain or discomfort. Wellness is much broader and better than that; it's a more holistic way of looking at your overall health and well-being. There are several branches, including emotional, spiritual, intellectual, physical, environmental, financial, occupational and social wellness. The combination and balance of these crucial ingredients is what can make life feel really good.

Boosting your wellness is something you can do every day as part of an ongoing process. By making simple changes in different areas of your life you will start to see the benefits. Rather than presenting you with a fixed list of "things you must do", this book is designed to give you a range of suggestions that you can pick and choose at will, depending on what works best for you. And sprinkled between the tips are some inspirational quotes to offer further wisdom as you pursue a life that's packed with positivity. Be well!

There is only one corner
of the universe you can
be certain of improving,
and that's your own self.

Aldous Huxley

FIT IN FITNESS

Getting active every day will bring you obvious – and brilliant – physical benefits: strengthening your bones and muscles, boosting your immune system and reducing your risk of heart disease and other illnesses. It's also a great stress-buster, and as your fitness levels rise, so does your self-confidence.

Aim for 30 minutes of activity a day, but remember that you can split this up into two or three sessions if it's easier – and you don't need to break the bank to do it. How about a brisk 10-minute walk to and then from work, plus 10 minutes of sit-ups, squats and star jumps in front of your favourite TV show to get your 30-minute fix?

If you've time for a regular fitness class there are dozens of different things you can try your hand (and legs!) at, from hula-hooping to mixed martial arts. Take to the internet or check out your local sports centre to get some ideas.

THE GREATEST WEALTH IS HEALTH.

Virgil

Continuous
improvement is better
than delayed perfection.

Mark Twain

MAKE REFLECTION A ROUTINE

Set aside some time every day that's just for you – to reflect, meditate or write in your journal. Even if it's just 10 minutes before you go to bed, making "me time" a regular part of your routine is essential for boosting your wellness. It allows you to look back over your day and get to know your inner self a little better. You could even use the time to explore your spirituality with a podcast or book.

The more you praise
and celebrate your
life, the more there is
in life to celebrate.

Oprah Winfrey

LAUGH A LOT

Have you ever noticed how good you feel after laughing? Funny incidents and anecdotes obviously entertain us and leave us feeling happier, but the act of laughing has other brilliant benefits too, including reducing stress, relieving pain and improving our immune system. But it doesn't end there; sharing a joke connects us with others and helps us to put our troubles in perspective. Seek out humour every day – with your friends, in books, on TV or on stage – and enjoy the restorative effects of a good giggle.

A **smile** is a curve
that sets everything
straight.

Phyllis Diller

WRITE IT DOWN

Getting your thoughts down on paper is a tried-and-trusted method for improving your emotional well-being. Invest in a journal and write in it every day. If you need to offload your worries, writing them down before bed can improve your sleep, but try to include positivity in your journal entries, too. Make a note of the best moments of your day, the things that you're grateful for or which made you smile, and you'll have a mood-boosting record to look back on.

I can shake off
everything if I write;
my sorrows disappear,
my courage is reborn.

Anne Frank

SLOW IT DOWN OUTSIDE

The benefits of spending time outdoors are undeniable, from the physical boost of being outside in the fresh air and natural daylight, to the de-stressing effects of experiencing nature first-hand. A walk outdoors gives us a chance to get some perspective on our problems, too, so head outside on your lunch break or plan a trip to a local nature haven and you'll soon feel relaxed and reinvigorated.

You can make your outdoor adventure even more special by slowing it down and taking a moment to enjoy your surroundings, rather than just powering through them on a speedy hike or bike ride. If you can, wander off the beaten track and settle down quietly to watch and listen. The environment will soon come to life around you and you might experience a magical wildlife encounter or two.

Often we look so long at
the closed door that we
do not see the one which
has been opened for us.

Helen Keller

Better than a
thousand hollow
words, is one word
that brings **peace**.

Buddha

GET GROUNDED

Grounding is a wonderful spiritual practice that reminds us of our connection with the planet and helps us to draw on its healing energy. The simplest way to ground yourself is to walk barefoot on the grass. Then stand for a few moments and breathe slowly, feeling your connection with the earth beneath your feet and letting healing energy flow up into you from below. Try it daily if you can; it's great for those moments when you feel flighty and unable to concentrate.

The goal of life is to
make your heartbeat
match the beat of the
universe, to match your
nature with Nature.

Joseph Campbell

TAKE A TRIP

Travel broadens the mind and gives us a break from our everyday lives. You don't have to backpack around the world to get the benefits of a trip away, but experiencing a new culture can be wonderfully inspiring and rewarding. If you're a homebody, you could visit a local site and appreciate your environment with fresh eyes. But if you're ready for a more exotic adventure, try visiting somewhere different on your next vacation and you'll enjoy a boost that will long outlive your trip.

The world's **big** and I want to have a **good** look at it before it gets dark.

John Muir

LEARN A LANGUAGE

It's important to look after our intellectual well-being by learning new skills. MRI scans of the brain have shown that language learning increases our cognitive abilities and creativity, too. It's also good fun: there are plenty of language apps available to get you started, and there's a supportive learning community to be tapped into online. Once you've got a few key phrases under your belt, you can reward yourself with a trip abroad to try out your new skills.

We must believe that
we are gifted for
something, and that
this thing, at whatever
cost, must be attained.

Marie Curie

ACT OR DISTRACT

Life is precious, so don't spend a minute longer than necessary brooding over things. If you feel you've been treated unfairly, speak up (once you've had time to think things over calmly) and then move on. The only person who will suffer if you let resentments simmer away is yourself, so once you've expressed your feelings (on paper if not in person), make a positive choice to focus on something completely different – and fun – until any past hurts start to fade.

A lot of people are afraid to say what they want. That's why they don't get what they want.

Madonna

The best way to
predict your future
is to **create** it.

Anonymous

Health is more than
the absence of disease.
Health is about jobs and
employment, education,
the environment, and all
of those things that go
into making us healthy.

Joycelyn Elders

MEDITATE

Meditation needn't be complicated, and by learning how to quieten your mind and find stillness every day, you'll improve your physical, emotional and spiritual well-being no end. The simplest way to start is by spending a couple of minutes sitting quietly and focusing on your breathing. You can do this anywhere, but if you have a corner of your home that you can turn into a comfy meditation space, all the better.

First take a moment to relax, becoming aware of any areas of tension in your body and releasing them. Then direct your attention to your breathing – a slow, deep breath in through the nose, followed by a long breath out through your mouth. Stay focused on the sound and rhythm of your breath, setting aside any distracting thoughts that come to mind. (Meditation is not about stopping your thoughts, but simply learning to let them come and go, without getting caught up in them.)

With practice you'll find that you can focus for a little longer each time. You may find calming music or a guided meditation track a useful addition to your meditation routine.

WHATEVER YOU DO, BE DIFFERENT.

Anita Roddick

Imagination is
more important than
knowledge. Knowledge
is limited. Imagination
encircles the world.

Albert Einstein

LOOK AFTER YOUR GUT

So much of our well-being stems from us having a healthy gut. The helpful bacteria in your gut affect your immune system and your mood as well as control the absorption of nutrients from your food, so it's vital to boost these bacteria through your diet. Including a variety of whole foods is a great start, but you can go one step further by including fermented foods, such as miso and kimchi, and cultured dairy products. Include cabbage, mushrooms and onions in your meals and try a probiotic supplement, too.

Take care of your body. It's the only place you have to live.

Jim Rohn

GET INSPIRED, THEN GET CREATIVE

Doing something creative is both relaxing and rewarding, so why not explore your creativity with a project that takes its inspiration from an existing piece of art. Visit a museum or gallery and focus on an exhibit that particularly interests you. Spend some time pondering what appeals to you about your chosen piece and take some photos (if allowed). Use this as inspiration to create your own artwork using whichever medium you like. You could paint a picture, write a poem or display your photographs.

Nothing is impossible;
the word itself says
"I'm possible"!

Audrey Hepburn

VOLUNTEER

One of the best ways to boost your mood and self-esteem is to do something that makes you feel worthwhile – and volunteering is a great option. Perhaps you have skills and knowledge that you can use to help others? Or maybe you're passionate about wildlife or an environmental cause and could support this locally.

One of the most valuable gifts you can give, however, is your time and attention. Many people are unable to get out and about, so spending an hour or so each week with someone like this can transform their life… and yours, too. Check online for charities which run schemes where you can either visit someone housebound or give them a weekly friendship call, or simply think of someone you know who might benefit from a regular visit and you running an errand or two for them.

Making contact with others and helping them in this way will mean that you feel connected and valued, and you'll be boosting someone else's well-being at the same time.

Health is a state of
complete **harmony**
of the body, mind
and **spirit**.

B. K. S. Iyengar

You can be whoever
you choose to become
in the future.

Lady Gaga

SET UP A SAVING GOAL

If you'd like to treat yourself to something, make small savings throughout the week to stash away the cash. Put the coins you would've spent on non-essentials into a jar and watch your fund mount up. Buying your usual coffee and sandwich every day can be expensive, so why not make yourself a packed lunch and take a flask of coffee to enjoy outside instead? Once you've hit your target, you can savour your treat and the satisfaction of having saved up for it, too.

Beware of little
expenses. A small leak
will sink a **great** ship.

Benjamin Franklin

WORK POSITIVE

It's important to feel valued at work, but if you often feel unhappy, take steps to improve things. It's your responsibility to sort things out – and doing so will benefit your mental and physical well-being, too. Think about what isn't working in your current role and how it could be improved. Talk to your boss to see if things can change; if not, plan to move on – even if this means a new start. You spend most of your week at work, so make sure it's a positive place to be.

If you feel underwhelmed by your current occupation, but unsure what you could do instead, try out an online careers questionnaire. (Those that assess your personality type and then suggest vocations based on this are very interesting.) Careers fairs are also a great source of inspiration. It may be possible to get some work experience in a different sector, or to take advantage of flexible working arrangements to combine different roles, or to develop a hobby into a money-spinner alongside your day job. Be open-minded and see where your interests lead you.

In a disordered mind,
as in a disordered
body, soundness of
health is impossible.

Cicero

A SELF THAT GOES ON CHANGING IS A SELF THAT GOES ON LIVING.

Virginia Woolf

LIVE IN HARMONY WITH THE PLANET

Nurturing our connection with the environment is an important aspect of wellness. We are all living beings and part of the earth's ecosphere. We have adapted to thrive in our environment and respond to the rhythms of the natural world. If we can't do these things, we can never truly be happy.

Getting outside as often as possible is one way to connect with nature, but actively doing something to benefit the environment or the habitats around us is rewarding, too. Help out with a local environmental or wildlife cause if you can – one that gets you out and about and experiencing the landscape around you.

You could also think about starting your own environmental campaign: could you set up a recycling scheme at work? Or take action to minimize the use of plastics in your home? Even litter-picking or putting out seed and water for your local wildlife can enhance your connection with the planet we call home.

The only person you
are **destined** to
become is the person
you **decide** to be.

Ralph Waldo Emerson

We are what we
repeatedly do.

Will Durant

HONOUR YOUR INTUITION

Learn to tune in to your intuition and you'll find yourself making the choices that most closely reflect your true feelings. We often use the expression "going with your gut", and it's true that our physical reactions to different situations – and people – can reveal a lot about our values. Once you recognize your inner voice, trust that it has your best interests at heart and have the confidence to follow the path that's best for you.

Don't set **sail** using someone else's **star**.

African proverb

PICK A PODCAST

Podcasts are a wonderful way of expanding your knowledge, which – the World Health Organization has shown – will have a positive impact on your mental well-being and can guard against dementia, too. You can use podcasts to learn more about the world, to discover more about yourself or to enjoy a get-away-from-it-all moment on your lunch break. A quick online search will help you discover the most popular podcasts in your favourite genre, or you can ask around for recommendations.

To live is the rarest
thing in the world. Most
people exist, that is all.

Oscar Wilde

VISIT A MIND, BODY AND SPIRIT EVENT

If you've never given much thought to exploring your spiritual side, it can be difficult to know where to start, but there are many wonderful spiritual practices you can try. A good place to begin is at a Mind, Body and Spirit festival, an event which brings together different practitioners under one roof, offering taster sessions in dozens of different disciplines – often for free. Try out anything and everything, and you'll come away with plenty of ideas on how to include spiritual self-care in your life.

That's life: starting over,
one breath at a time.

Sharon Salzberg

No matter what
the **situation,**
remind yourself
"I have a **choice**".

Deepak Chopra

IF NOT NOW, WHEN?

WHEN?

Hillel the Elder

BUILD POSITIVE RELATIONSHIPS

Our relationships with those around us have a huge impact on our well-being, so it's important to nurture the positives and work on – or break free from – any negative connections. Make time for regular catch-ups with friends and family – the people who leave you feeling positive and happy. Be sure that it's quality time you spend together, too. Sharing a meal or an activity will make your interactions more mindful and meaningful.

Not all of our relationships with others are positive, though, and it's important to work out a strategy for dealing with these. Minimize contact with anyone who leaves you feeling drained or stressed. If these are connections you need to maintain, see if you can find ways to improve them, and at the very least make sure you don't take on board anyone else's negativity. Remind yourself that, if people behave badly toward you, it's not a reflection on you, so don't dwell on these tricky, less-than-positive moments. Focus on the cheerful encounters and enjoy them wholeheartedly; don't give the negative ones too much thinking space.

EMBRACE ACCEPTANCE

If you get worked up over situations which haven't panned out as you'd hoped, your frustrations will take over your day and impact on your well-being. Instead, try to accept things you can't change and stop dwelling on the alternative outcome. (This can take a little work, but is far less difficult than fighting against circumstances that are beyond your control.) So if you can't change something, change the way you respond to it. Look for the positives and focus on those – or on something else entirely.

Everything in
our life should be
based on love.

Ray Bradbury

PAMPER YOURSELF

A little pampering benefits your mind and body, and by recreating your favourite spa treatments at home you can treat yourself whenever you like. Take a relaxing bath at least once a week. Bathing gives you time to take stock, listen to music, read a book and maybe even sip a favourite drink. It also regulates the body's circadian rhythms, which stabilize mood and prepare you for a better night's sleep. Add your favourite bath products or essential oils for a touch of luxury or some rock salt for a detox, and don't forget to set the scene by lighting some candles.

You could include face and body treatments in your bathing ritual, too: why not make your own face mask (with some mashed banana); treat yourself to a pedicure or try out some self-massage or acupressure. These are all simple techniques and there are plenty of online tutorials to guide you, so make time to nurture yourself and enjoy the feelings of positivity and relaxation you get as a result.

When we are ready
to make positive
changes in our lives,
we attract whatever
we need to help us.

Louise Hay

The only way to be
truly **satisfied** is to
do what you believe
is **great** work.

Steve Jobs

BRING THE OUTSIDE IN

For days when you're just too busy for a walk outside, bring nature to yourself in any way that you can. Open the window to feel the breeze, have a picture of your favourite nature haven as your screensaver and add a pot plant to your office or home. Studies have shown that plants with a high transpiration rate – such as peace lilies and spider plants – add moisture to the air and can even benefit your skin. Plants also oxygenate the air, too.

If you take care of
the small things, the
big things take care
of themselves.

Emily Dickinson

LEARN TO DEAL WITH STRESS

Everyone experiences stress – it's a natural reaction to new experiences and the pressures of everyday life; but too much can affect your mental and physical well-being, so learning to deal with it is an essential skill when you're working toward wellness. Try out meditation, yoga and breathing techniques to see what works best for you and make time to include a short session every day. (There are simple versions of all these practices which can be mastered very easily with online tutorials, so don't feel you need to take classes or spend lots of time learning the ropes before you feel the effects.)

Remember also that you can learn to respond to negative situations differently and you can, in effect, choose to feel less stressed about the things you can't control. Try guided meditations that help you visualize your worries floating away, and explore mindfulness techniques to bring your attention to the present rather than dwelling on past niggles or worrying about what-ifs.

A great hallmark of
mental wellness is the
ability to be in the
present moment, fully
and with no thoughts
of being elsewhere.

Wayne Dyer

Love **all**, trust a **few**,
do wrong to **none**.

William Shakespeare

FIX IT

It's all too easy to soldier on when we have aches, pains or niggles, but choosing to live an actively healthy life means making time to look after ourselves if something's wrong. If you've been putting off checking out physical symptoms or if you think you may be struggling with a tricky emotional or relationship problem, take positive steps to get it sorted now. Get a friend on board for moral support and take action; you'll feel much better for tackling it head on.

YOU HAVE THE RIGHT TO LIVE A BEAUTIFUL LIFE.

Selena Gomez

CHANGE YOUR ATTITUDE TO NUTRITION

Rather than seeing a healthy diet as restrictive, change your thinking about what you eat and embrace a positive and proactive attitude to your food choices. Food has a huge impact on us – both physically and mentally. Your diet affects everything from your mood and stress levels to how alert you feel, how well you sleep and how comfortable you are after a meal. It can also be responsible for digestive discomfort, skin conditions, joint pain, bad breath and autoimmune reactions, among other things.

If you suffer from any minor ailments there's bound to be something you can do to tweak your diet to help, and you may even experience a turnaround in your symptoms. Look into nutritional "superfoods" or do some online research around your condition. (You should, of course, always consult your medical professional if you're concerned about your health.)

THINK POSITIVE

Make an effort to look on the bright side and you can train your brain to react positively rather than negatively to life's challenges. It takes a little practice at first, but if you can find something positive to focus on when things don't go your way, you'll soon become a glass-half-full kind of person. An optimistic outlook leaves you feeling happier and less stressed, and builds self-confidence. You'll find yourself taking on challenges with a positive attitude and ultimately getting better results.

If you want to

be happy, be.

Leo Tolstoy

PUZZLE IT OUT

If you challenge your brain regularly with puzzles, you'll improve your concentration, memory and problem-solving skills. You'll also de-stress and build your confidence at the same time. There are a whole plethora of puzzles out there to try – whether you choose word games, logic problems or number puzzles. You could even get together with friends to tackle an escape room. Look for fun and absorbing ways to build your brain power and you're certain to find something that appeals to you.

Be happy with being
you. Love your flaws.
Own your quirks.

Ariana Grande

Positive **anything**
is better than negative
nothing.

Elbert Hubbard

Let us be grateful to people who make us happy; they are the charming gardeners who make our souls blossom.

Marcel Proust

KNOW YOUR NEEDS

Getting to know your own social needs is a crucial part of enjoying a happy and rewarding social life, and this will impact on all your other areas of wellness. It's important to remember that everyone is different, so don't feel that you should be out and about socializing every evening if that just doesn't work for you. Many of us are introverts and find that a quick trip to the coffee shop will keep our social life ticking over for a few days, or know that we need a little downtime after a big social event.

If you haven't thought much about this before, try keeping a mood-tracking journal and work out when you need a little time to yourself – or conversely a little more social time – to promote your well-being. Then make your plans accordingly and don't feel guilty if they don't match up with other people's ideas. What you feel is right for you is right for you, and that's just fine.

PARADISE IS TO LOVE MANY THINGS WITH A PASSION.

Pablo Picasso

Life shrinks or
expands in proportion
to one's courage.

Anaïs Nin

BE YOUR OWN BEST FRIEND

Your wellness is your responsibility, so make the most of every opportunity you get to treat yourself kindly. Practise being your own best friend by making sure your self-talk is positive and by rewarding yourself when you can. If you feel you've messed up, remind yourself that we all make mistakes. If you're feeling drained, treat yourself to a massage. If you struggle with stress, find moments of mindfulness in your day. Be kind to yourself and you'll immediately feel happier and more confident.

Talk to **yourself**
like you would to
someone you **love**.

Brené Brown

MEET UP WITH YOUR FRIENDS

Spending time with our friends provides a brilliant wellness boost, as it reminds us that we're part of something greater – a group with shared memories, ideas and laughter. But to enjoy the benefits of your nearest and dearest, you have to make time to meet up with them! Set up a regular meet if you can, or take the initiative and organize a trip together, a night in with a pizza or even just a speedy coffee before work.

Make a conscious effort
to surround yourself
with positive, nourishing
and uplifting people.

Jack Canfield

SPROUT SOME SEEDS

You probably already know the benefits of including seeds in your diet – they're powerhouses of protein, fibre, vitamins and minerals – but did you know that you can sprout your seeds for added nutrients and flavour? You can sprout beans, grains and some veggie seeds in the same way that you grow cress. The sprouts will add a different texture to salads and sandwiches, and all you need is a jam jar.

Punch a few holes in the lid of your jar and rinse around two tablespoons of seeds in cool water. Then pop them into your jar, cover with a couple of inches of cool water and let them soak for around 8 hours. Drain well (through the lid of your jar), rinse carefully and soak again, repeating this process for two to three days until the seeds are fully sprouted. Rinse and drain thoroughly before eating (or store in the fridge for several days). Have fun experimenting with different sprouts, including radish, chickpea, sunflower seeds and lentils.

THERE
ARE ALWAYS
FLOWERS FOR
THOSE WHO
WANT TO
SEE THEM.

Henri Matisse

Every day brings a chance for you to draw in a breath, kick off your shoes... and dance.

Oprah Winfrey

TRY A NEW HOBBY

Taking on a different challenge, such as a new hobby or activity, will improve your wellness across the board, increasing your happiness and confidence levels, and benefitting you socially, intellectually, mentally and physically. If you're unsure where to start, pick up an activity you enjoyed as a child, or try something completely new that's always piqued your interest. Art, writing, archery, circus skills... the choice is yours. It's always fun to experiment – if you don't enjoy it, just give something else a go.

Anybody can do anything; it's up to themselves. All it takes is the right intentions.

Jimi Hendrix

WORKPLACE WELLNESS

Look for ways in which you can improve your wellness at work and your ideas may help others, too. Some areas where you may be able to encourage improvements are:

Could you brighten up your surroundings with plants or wall art? Can you add comfortable touches to break areas? Could an outdoor space be set up with a bench or two? Can you campaign for healthy snacks instead of a vending machine?

Would a weekly lunch together improve morale? How about a new work tradition like taking turns to bake on a Friday or setting up a running club? The Scandinavian tradition of everyone sharing a quick coffee break and chat (*fika*) is worth embracing, too.

Could you suggest having "walking meetings" outside? Or raise awareness of how regular short breaks improve concentration? Could your workplace host a weekly yoga or meditation class? (If you provided stats on how this would benefit productivity, the "powers that be" might be interested!) Could you have some face-to-face conversations (and build relationships with your colleagues) instead of generating masses of emails?

We should not feel
embarrassed by our
difficulties, only by our
failure to grow anything
beautiful from them.

Alain de Botton

Always stay true to **yourself** and never let what somebody says distract you from your **goals**.

Michelle Obama

GATHER UP GRATITUDE

Focusing on challenges that need our attention every day can make us forget to appreciate the good things we experience too. Reflect on your day and appreciate its blessings, however small. Keeping a gratitude journal is one way to do this, but you can capture these special moments in any way you like – from sharing a photo of a beautiful sunset to logging the day's funniest moments on a noticeboard. Reflecting on them will help you relive the happiness they brought you.

Expect the best.
Prepare for the
worst. Capitalize
on what comes.

Zig Ziglar

KEEP IT NATURAL

Eating for wellness isn't complicated. If you pick foods that are as natural as possible, with few additives, you'll feel the benefits. Think of your body as a machine and give it the fuel it was designed to digest to keep it in tip-top condition. Include as wide a range of fruits and vegetables as possible and prepare meals from scratch whenever you can. If you're buying pre-prepared, opt for items with fewer ingredients as these will generally be better for you.

One cannot think well,
love well, sleep well, if
one has not dined well.

Virginia Woolf

They always say **time** changes things, but you actually have to change them **yourself**.

Andy Warhol

It will never rain roses:
when we want to have
more roses, we must
plant more roses.

George Eliot

LET IT GO!

Bottling up negative (or positive!) feelings is a sure-fire cause of stress, frustration and unhappiness – so learn to release your feelings regularly, in a safe way, for a calmer and happier mindset every day. Tried-and-trusted methods such as chatting to a friend, writing down your feelings in a journal or releasing tension by exercising, dancing or singing will help you to let off some steam and prevent stresses from building up and affecting your everyday quality of life.

NATURE'S PEACE WILL FLOW INTO YOU AS THE SUNSHINE FLOWS INTO TREES.

John Muir

STAY HYDRATED

Dehydration can have an impact on your concentration levels and your physical well-being, causing headaches, dizziness and lethargy. It's a common side-effect of a busy lifestyle, but make the effort to regularly sip water throughout the day and you'll be surprised at how much more alert you'll feel. You're aiming for eight glasses of water a day, but herbal teas and fruit juice count, too. If you find you're constantly forgetting to drink, set an hourly reminder to refill your glass until you reach your target.

The best six doctors
anywhere – and no
one can deny it – are
sunshine, water, rest and
air, exercise and diet.

Anonymous

LEARN THAT LESS IS MORE

One of the most effective ways to improve your well-being is to simplify your life. Whether it's your belongings, your commitments or even your friendships, life is much easier and more rewarding when you embrace an attitude of "less is more". Decluttering your home is an obvious place to start, so target the area that bugs you most and have a 10-minute tidy. Keep only the things you really love or use regularly, rehoming anything that hasn't earned the right to be there.

Next, turn your attention to your time and look at ways to streamline that. See if you can cut out any unnecessary weekly commitments or perhaps share onerous duties with others. Practise saying no – politely but firmly – if you're asked to take on anything extra that you really don't want to do. Remember: it's up to you to value your time and use it wisely. Be proactive about this and you'll feel a lot less stressed, and able to commit fully to the things that make you happy.

FOCUS ON FAMILY

Like spending time with friends, being with our family is a great mood-booster and reminds us that we belong to a group of caring people with a shared history. Arrange or attend regular family gatherings and enjoy the feelings of happiness these inspire. You might even like to start a new family tradition, resurrect some board games or activities you enjoyed when you were younger, or organize a trip down memory lane together with some old photos.

Family is not an
important thing.
It's everything.

Michael J. Fox

SENSIBLE SWAPS

If the thought of completely overhauling your diet seems a little daunting, take it one step at a time. You could tackle a different area every week. Target sugar first and swap sweet treats for healthier options, such as fruit salad or berries. Next, why not trade white, processed flour products for wholemeal versions? Then cut down on salty foods, using herbs to add flavour to your meals instead. And finally replace high-fat cheeses or snacks with lower-fat versions. Don't forget to add in plenty of vegetables, nuts and pulses.

You'll feel more energized, sleep better and improve your overall health dramatically when you fine-tune your diet in this way. Even swapping one regular snack for a healthier version can help. Replace your usual bag of potato crisps with lightly salted popcorn; your can of soda with naturally flavoured water, or your daily chocolate bar with a square or two of dark chocolate.

What soap is to the
body, laughter
is to the **soul**.

Yiddish proverb

The present moment
is filled with joy and
happiness. If you are
attentive, you will see it.

Thích Nhất Hạnh

TAKE A BREAK
FROM TECH

Having a day where you take some time out from technology will benefit your mind, body and spirit. If you can, turn off your phone for the day and either get out and about to enjoy nature or have a session catching up on your reading, your hobbies or spending time with friends. It's refreshing to give your mind a break from headlines, notifications and newsfeeds, allowing you to process everything you've experienced. It will help you de-stress, too.

NATURE IS NOT A PLACE TO VISIT. IT IS HOME.

Gary Snyder

SEE THE SIGNS

Be your own healer by keeping an eye out for signs that you may need to adjust your lifestyle or diet. Your nails are a great indicator of your health: strong nails with no flecks in them indicate a healthy diet, but if your nails are mis-shaped or flecked with white you may be suffering from an iron or zinc deficiency. Check out your symptoms and seek medical advice if you're at all worried.

Your tongue is also a good indicator of your health. In Ayurvedic medicine the tongue is used for diagnosis of all sorts of conditions. If yours has a layer of "bloom" it can indicate intolerances or toxicities and it may be time to overhaul your diet.

More generally, pay attention to what your body seems to be saying. Are you constantly tired? Gaining or losing weight? Afflicted by mood swings? These are your body's way of telling you that something isn't right. While this feedback may not be pleasant to receive or even acknowledge, try to see it as an opportunity to address any underlying issues.

The amount of
stress in your life is
determined by how
much energy you expend
resisting your life.

Gary Zukav

If you don't like something, **change** it. If you can't change it, change your **attitude**.

Maya Angelou

LIVE WITH PURPOSE

Developing a strong sense of purpose will make it much easier for you to stay positive and motivated, and to enjoy higher levels of self-esteem. But having purpose doesn't have to mean working toward a goal on a distant horizon or changing the person you are now. Instead, concentrate on living your life purposefully in the moment.

Contemplate the values that matter to you and honour these in the decisions you make every day. Think about the subjects and causes that speak to you, and study or pursue these in your spare time. Identify the most important elements in your day-to-day roles and carry them out with pride. If you're unsure of what these are, do some brainstorming around the roles you carry out: which duties or activities bring you the most satisfaction? Perhaps you're naturally an optimistic soul who can inspire your friends. Maybe you love being a nurturing parent or an organized co-worker.

By focusing on what you value most you can find a sense of meaning in your everyday activities straightaway, and steer your future plans in a direction that's ever more meaningful to you.

Physical fitness is
not only one of the
most important keys
to a healthy body,
it is the basis of
dynamic and creative
intellectual activity.

John F. Kennedy

Our mind is **enriched**
by what we receive, our
heart by what we **give**.

Victor Hugo

EXPLORE ENERGY PRACTICES

Nurture your spiritual self for greater mental and physical well-being. Trying a practice such as yoga, t'ai chi or reiki will teach you to work with the energy flow in your body (also known as *chi*). These calming practices offer you the opportunity to get in touch with your spiritual side and to cultivate an inner calmness and wellness over time; you'll also feel immediate benefits in terms of relaxation. Sign up for a taster session or look online for simple tutorials to get started.

Happiness is when what you think, what you say, and what you do are in harmony.

Mahatma Gandhi

SORT OUT YOUR FINANCES

Money worries are one of the most common reasons people experience stress. Improving your wellness is very much an active process, and sorting out your finances is certainly an area where you need to take the lead and tackle things head on – no one else will do it for you! The good news is that there are lots of free apps and online calculators to help you get your finances in order. Use one to draw up a summary of your incomings and outgoings and get a picture of where your money is being spent.

It's worth regularly checking through your expenses to see where you can save money. For each regular outgoing payment, think about whether it's something you really need and use: could you cut the cost of your gym membership or entertainments subscriptions, for example? If it is an essential item, shop around, search online and see if you can find a better deal. It may take a few hours, but you could save yourself a significant amount of money – and stress – by doing it.

FEAR IS ONLY AS DEEP AS THE MIND ALLOWS.

Japanese proverb

Every day we choose
who we are by how
we define ourselves.

Angelina Jolie

SLEEP WELL

In order to experience optimum well-being you need to get a good night's sleep... and in order to get a good night's sleep, you need to look after yourself! If you're stressed, unwell, not eating properly or not giving yourself enough downtime before bed, your sleep may suffer; establishing a relaxing bedtime routine is important. You may wish to avoid caffeinated drinks in the evening (and sugary or processed foods). Herbal teas – particularly those that contain valerian root – can be a great aid to sleep if you struggle to drop off.

A relaxing bath, yoga, meditation or breathing exercises, and some screen-free time before bed, are also tried-and-tested ways to help you unwind. Spending a few moments journaling and reflecting on the day can also be very rewarding. It may sound obvious but you won't enjoy a great night's sleep if you aren't comfortable, so invest in a good mattress (or mattress topper), adjust the lighting and temperature of your bedroom to suit you, and make sure that your room feels like a cosy haven without being cluttered with belongings or work paraphernalia.

Think in the morning.
Act in the noon.
Eat in the evening.
Sleep in the night.

William Blake

Success is not the key to happiness. Happiness is the key to success.

Albert Schweitzer

SEE DECISIONS AS OPPORTUNITIES

Pursuing wellness is a proactive process: you are in the driving seat, and have the power to improve your well-being every day. In fact, every decision you make is an opportunity, so consider your choices and pick options that will benefit you. That doesn't mean you *always* have to eat salad or go for a run rather than enjoying a box set – treats have a place in our happiness, too – but it *is* important to realize you're in control of your well-being and to relish the responsibility.

If you really want to do something you'll find a way. If you don't, you'll find an excuse.

Jim Rohn

SAY "NO" MORE

Life can often feel like a mad rush from one thing to the next, leaving us with little control over our time, but learning to say "no" is a vital way to safeguard your well-being. Turning down requests we don't have time for can feel difficult, but it's an important skill. Taking on too many commitments will leave you feeling overtired and unable to give your best, so practise declining requests politely and then enjoy giving your all to the things you do include in your day.

The oldest, shortest words – "yes" and "no" – are those which require the most thought.

Pythagoras

BREATHE BETTER

You may think that you've got breathing down to a fine art, but most of us can improve our technique for a positive effect on our physical and mental well-being. Focus on taking longer, deeper breaths into the depths of your lungs. Rest your hand on your diaphragm and feel it rise as you count in for four and then fall as you breathe out for four. Slower, steadier breathing will instantly help you to feel more relaxed and you'll feel more energized too, as you'll be oxygenating your blood more efficiently.

Concentrating on your breathing is also a valuable exercise in mindfulness as breathing exercises give you a focus in the present moment, stopping your mind from getting distracted by worries. Try to bring yourself back to short periods of calm, slow breathing regularly throughout the day to maximize the benefits. You could even set yourself a reminder on your phone to carry out your breathwork.

THE HAPPINESS OF YOUR LIFE DEPENDS UPON THE QUALITY OF YOUR THOUGHTS.

Marcus Aurelius

Do not lower your goals to the level of your abilities. Instead, raise your abilities to the height of your goals.

Swami Vivekananda

DISCUSS AND DEBATE

Discussions help us to consider our own values, form opinions and learn to appreciate other people's points of view. This is an important part of nurturing our intellectual well-being. If you're not ready for a full-on debate, read up on a topic that interests you and see if you can fit a conversation about it into your week. You could set up an informal discussion group with friends to chat about current events, or share ideas at a book or film club.

Great minds
discuss ideas;
average minds
discuss events;
small minds
discuss people.

Anonymous

MEET NEW PEOPLE

Interacting with a different group of people, even if it's just for an evening, can be a really positive experience. It's socially rewarding to build new connections and refreshing to hear new ideas and opinions. Also, when you're meeting people for the first time, you get a chance to introduce yourself anew – something you may not have done for a while – and you can learn a lot about your current self in this way.

Look for opportunities to meet or interact with new people whenever you can (as far as is comfortable for you). A short conversation with someone next to you in the queue at the coffee shop is a good start – you could try paying them a compliment to get the ball rolling. Or look for local events or meet-ups for people who share your hobbies and interests, such as a book group, a walking club or a gaming convention. These are all great opportunities to embrace new experiences and meet like-minded people, which will leave you feeling inspired, connected and valued.

The positive thinker
sees the invisible, feels
the intangible and
achieves the impossible.

Winston Churchill

IF YOU DON'T STEP FORWARD, YOU'RE ALWAYS IN THE SAME PLACE.

Nora Roberts

KEEP SMILING

Start every day with the intention of beaming out positivity to the people you meet. When you have conversations with your friends or colleagues, radiate acceptance and understanding. If you decide to enter into all your interactions with a feeling of love and respect, you'll be amazed at how it changes other people's reactions to you. Even the simple act of smiling at others can add warmth and happiness to your day, so give it a try.

Keep smiling because
life is a **beautiful**
thing and there's so
much to **smile** about.

Marilyn Monroe

HAVE AN EMERGENCY PLAN

Some times in our lives are more stressful than others, and having a plan to help you get through difficult times will ensure that you cope as well as you can – and that your wellness doesn't take too much of a battering – when you're under pressure. It's good to have something written down for when you need it, so make some lists in your journal.

Who can you turn to in times of trouble? (Write down the names of your "support group" and their attributes.) What are your priorities and values? (Writing these down can be useful if you have to make a difficult decision.) Where are your favourite spots to relax? What are your top five de-stressing activities? Which YouTube clips, films, songs or books cheer you up if you're down?

You might also like to have an emergency de-stressing routine all ready and prepared for the end of a difficult day: it could be a relaxing candlelit bath, a cup of herbal tea, a meditation track or some yoga stretches, followed by a session of reading or journaling in bed.

Your present
circumstances don't
determine where
you can go; they
merely determine
where you start.

Nido Qubein